FOREWORD

Improvised explosive devices and car bombs have long been identified as threats to U.S. Army personnel deployed in Iraq and Afghanistan. They have gained considerable attention and notoriety, even infamy, among our troops, who have had to learn the appropriate responses and countermeasures to contend with the fielding of these systems against them. Far less recognized is the fact that a similar threat—embodied in car bombs—has emerged much closer to our homeland within Mexico. Since mid-2010, cartel car bombings have taken place in a country on our southern border and have been targeted against both the forces of opposing cartels and those belonging to Mexican military and law enforcement agencies.

With the election of the new presidential Institutional Revolutionary Party (PRI) administration in July 2012, these car bombings have ceased altogether after rapidly escalating in their levels of employment. Whether this was a response to the expected shift in countercartel policies from the National Action Party (PAN) to the PRI administration that began in December 2012, simply a "strategic pause" of some sort, or an outcome of another casual factor is unknown. What is important is that the use of car bombs in Mexico by the cartels has the potential to threaten U.S. agents, facilities, and interests in that nation and could also conceivably spread to our border cities—though this would appear to be a very unlikely possibility based on the use of car bomb trends and analysis presented in this Paper.

The authors of this Letort Paper, Dr. Robert Bunker and John Sullivan, draw upon their wealth of knowledge and expertise pertaining to the Mexican cartels and organized crime and, interestingly, is derived from their long-standing counterterrorism backgrounds with regard to suicide bombing and active aggressor response. Furthermore, they are able to look at the context in which cartel car bombings are taking place in Mexico from both military (counterinsurgency) and policing (counter high intensity crime) perspectives. As a result, this Paper is useful and important not only for U.S. Army interests and concerns—including that of domestic force protection implications—but also because of its analytical implications concerning interpreting indications and warnings events that develop actionable strategic intelligence requirements.

The Strategic Studies Institute hopes the findings and recommendations provided in this manuscript will be of interest to the broader U.S strategic community and the U.S. Army organizations engaged in providing support to the various agencies and commands belonging to the federal government of the Mexican state.

DOUGLAS C. LOVELACE, JR.
Director
Strategic Studies Institute and
 U.S. Army War College Press

ABOUT THE AUTHORS

ROBERT J. BUNKER is a Distinguished Visiting Professor and Minerva Chair at the Strategic Studies Institute, U.S. Army War College. He is also Adjunct Faculty, School of Politics and Economics, Claremont Graduate University. Past professional associations include Futurist in Residence, Training and Development Division, Behavioral Science Unit, Federal Bureau of Investigation Academy, Quantico, VA; CEO, Counter-OPFOR Corporation; Adjunct Faculty, School of Policy, Planning, and Development, University of Southern California; Terrorism Instructor, California Specialized Training Institute, California Office of Emergency Services; Staff Member (Consultant), Counter-OPFOR Program, National Law Enforcement and Corrections Technology Center-West; Fellow, Institute of Land Warfare, Association of the U.S. Army; Adjunct Faculty, National Security Studies M.A. Program and Political Science Department, California State University, San Bernardino, CA; and Faculty, Unconventional Warfare M.A. Distance Education Program, American Military University. Dr. Bunker has delivered over 200 presentations, including papers and training, to military, law enforcement, and academic and policy audiences, including U.S. congressional testimony. He has over 200 publications ranging from edited books and booklets to reports, chapters, articles/essays, response guidance, subject bibliographies, and encyclopedia entries in academic, policy, military, and law enforcement venues. Among those are *Red Teams and Counterterrorism Training*, with Stephen Sloan (University of Oklahoma, 2011), and edited works, including *Criminal Insurgencies in Mexico and the Americas: The Gangs and Cartels Wage War*

(Routledge, 2012); *Narcos Over the Border: Gangs, Cartels and Mercenaries* (Routledge, 2011); *Criminal-States and Criminal-Soldiers* (Routledge, 2008); *Networks, Terrorism and Global Insurgency* (Routledge, 2005); and *Non-State Threats and Future Wars* (Routledge, 2002). Dr. Bunker holds university degrees in political science, government, social science, anthropology-geography, behavioral science, and history.

JOHN P. SULLIVAN is a career police officer. He currently serves as a lieutenant with the Los Angeles Sheriff's Department. He is also an Adjunct Researcher at the Vortex Foundation; Senior Research Fellow at the Center for Advanced Studies on Terrorism; Senior Fellow at the Stephenson Disaster Management Institute, Louisiana State University; and Senior Fellow at *Small Wars Journal-El Centro*. Mr. Sullivan is co-editor of *Countering Terrorism and WMD: Creating a Global Counter-Terrorism Network* (Routledge, 2006), and *Global Biosecurity: Threats and Responses* (Routledge, 2010). He is co-author of *Mexico's Criminal Insurgency: A Small Wars Journal-El Centro Anthology* (iUniverse, 2012). His current research focus is the impact of transnational organized crime on sovereignty in Mexico and other countries. Mr. Sullivan holds a bachelor of arts in government from the College of William and Mary and a master of arts in urban affairs and policy analysis from the New School for Social Research (Milano School).

Note: Both authors have benefited from past involvement with a multiyear suicide bomber research project for a national law enforcement center focusing on terrorist group use patterns, an initial study of the first year of suicide bombings that took place during Operation IRAQI FREEDOM, and training and exercises involving improvised explosive devices and car bomb threats in the Los Angeles County operational area.

SUMMARY

Contemporary Mexican cartel use of car bombs began in mid-July 2010, and their use has since escalated. Not only was their significance downplayed by the administration of former Mexican president Felipe Calderón, but they were basically ignored in the September 2010 State of the Nation Report (*informe*). As one co-author has noted, the July 15, 2010, Ciudad Juárez car bombing represents a firebreak in terms of "an apparently significant acceleration of tactics, techniques, and procedures (TTP)" for Mexican cartel violence. Given the escalatory nature of these bombings to the conflict taking place in Mexico, and indeed the close proximity of them to the United States — some literally within miles of the border — they should be of at least some interest to local, state, and federal U.S. law enforcement and, ultimately, to the U.S. Army and other governmental institutions, which are increasingly providing support to Mexican federal agencies.

With this in mind, this Paper first seeks to provide an historical overview and analysis of cartel car bomb use in Mexico. In doing so, it provides context, insights, and lessons learned stemming from the Medellin and Cali cartel car bombing campaigns that plagued Colombia, primarily between 1988 and 1993. It then discusses the initial cartel car bombings that took place in Mexico in the early 1990s — car bombings that most researchers have overlooked — before highlighting indications and warnings (I&W) events identified in the years prior to the resumption of Mexican cartel car bombings in mid-2010. Contemporary car bombings in Mexico from mid-2010 through much of 2012 will then be discussed and analyzed. Second, this Paper capitalizes on the historical overview and analysis provided — from both the Mexican and earlier Colombian experiences — in order to generate insights into future cartel car bombing potentials in Mexico. The identification of such potentials, in one sense, offers us a glimpse into cartel "enemy intent" — a possible form of actionable strategic intelligence.

An analysis of car bombing incidents in Mexico, with about 20 incidents identified over the last 2 1/2 years, is then provided. Both primary and secondary use patterns are discussed, along with future car bombing potentials in Mexico and the United States. For Mexico, steady, and both slowly increasing and quickly increasing car bomb use trajectories may exist. The prognosis for decreasing car bomb deployment currently appears unlikely. On the other hand, car cartel bomb use, at least on U.S. soil and directed at U.S. governmental personnel operating in Mexico, is presently far from a likely potential. If cartel car bombs were to be eventually deployed on U.S. soil or against U.S. personnel and facilities in Mexico, such as our consulates, we could expect that a pattern of I&W would be evident prior to such an attack or attacks. In that case, I&W would be drawn from precursor events such as grenade and improvised explosive device (IED) attacks (or attempted attacks) on our personnel and facilities and on evolving cartel car bomb deployment patterns in Mexico, especially concerning increases in tactical lethality and a shift toward anti-infrastructure targeting.

The authors of this monograph conclude with initial recommendations for U.S. Army and defense community support to a) the military and the federal, state, and local police agencies of the Mexican state; and b) the various U.S. federal, state, and local police agencies operating near the U.S.-Mexican border. Four thematic areas — intelligence, organization, training, and equipment — are highlighted, and the extent of these forms of support that may be provided should be situationally derived to counter cartel vehicle-borne IEDs and overall cartel threats. Additionally, a reappraisal of the Posse Comitatus Act of 1878 — enacted in a far different domestic security environment bereft of armed and organized nonstate threat entities able to challenge states — is said to be required if we are to lift some legal restrictions on U.S. military support to U.S. law enforcement agencies.

Further, the authors see the challenges posed by cartel *sicarios* (gunman; essentially nonstate soldiers) to be a hemispheric security challenge. In addition to internal U.S. military efforts and U.S. support to Mexican military (both the Mexican Secretariat of National Defense [SEDENA] and the Mexican Secretariat of the Navy [SEMAR]) and law enforcement (at all levels: federal, state, and municipal), support should also be extended to Central American states facing cartel and gang challenges. Ultimately, they contend that a comprehensive U.S. Northern Command (US-NORTHCOM) strategy should be developed in coordination with the Mexican government that integrates all elements of national power to mitigate and counter Mexican cartel use of car bombs and other forms of violence and corruption, manifesting themselves in Mexico and increasingly in the United States. To best serve U.S. national interests, however, this comprehensive strategy should also be integrated with the U.S. Southern Command (USSOUTHCOM) to create a Western Hemispheric strategy to combat gang, cartel, and other criminal insurgent threats to the Americas.

GLOSSARY

AfPak	Afghanistan-Pakistan
ARNORTH	U.S. Army North
C-4	Composition C (Plastic Explosive)
CBRNE	Chemical, Biological, Radiological, Nuclear, or Explosive
CISEN	Center for Research and National Security (*Centro de Investigación y Seguridad Nacional*)
COIN	Counterinsurgency
COTS	Commercial Off-The-Shelf
DAS	Administrative Department of Security (*Departamento Administradora de Seguridad en Proceso de Supresión*)
DEA	Drug Enforcement Administration
DHS	Department of Homeland Security
DIME	Diplomatic, Intelligence, Military, and Economic
DIME-P	Diplomatic, Intelligence, Military, Economic and Police
EMS	Emergency Medical Services
EOD	Explosive Ordnance Disposal
FARP	Armed Revolutionary Front of the People (*Fuerzas Armadas Revolucionarias del Pueblo*)
FBI	Federal Bureau of Investigation
FMSO	Foreign Military Studies Office
FY	Fiscal Year

GTD	Global Terrorism Database
IAB	InterAgency Board
I&W	Indications & Warnings
IED	Improvised Explosive Device
JIEDDO	Joint IED Defeat Organization
LAHIDTA	Los Angeles High Intensity Drug Trafficking Area
LAW	Light Anti-tank Weapon
LVB	Large Vehicle Bomb
MACTAC	Multi-Assault Counter-Terrorism Action Capabilities
MTT	Mobile Training Team
NGIC	National Ground Intelligence Center
OODA	Observe, Orient, Decide, and Act
OPFOR	Opposition Force
OPSEC	Operational Security
OSINT	Open Source Intelligence
UXO	Unexploded Ordnance
PAN	National Action Party (*Partido Acción Nacional*)
PGR	Office of the General Prosecutor (*Procuraduría General de la República*)
PRI	Institutional Revolutionary Party (*Partido Revolucionario Institucional*)
RAND	Research and Development
RDWTI	RAND Database of Worldwide Terrorism Incidents
RPG	Rocket Propelled Grenade
SEDENA	Secretariat of National Defense (*Secretaría de la Defensa Nacional*)

SEMAR	Naval Secretariat (*Secretaría de Marina*)
SMEE	Subject Matter Expert Exchanges
SWAT	Special Weapons and Tactics
TRADOC	Training and Doctrine Command
TTP	Tactics, Techniques, and/or Procedures
USAISC	U.S. Army Intelligence and Security Command
USNORTHCOM	U.S. Northern Command
USSOUTHCOM	U.S. Southern Command
VBIED	Vehicle Borne Improvised Explosive Device

CARTEL CAR BOMBINGS IN MEXICO

In early September 2010, President Felipe Calderón delivered a relatively upbeat annual State of the Nation Report (*informe*) concerning the nearly 4-year long war being waged across Mexico against the narco gangs, cartels, and mercenaries.[1] Simply put, the crackdown on organized crime was said to be working. Examples of success included killing and capturing about two dozen drug kingpins and firing about 3,200 Federal police officers — about 9 percent of the total force — in an effort to root out corruption and raise professional standards. Additionally, 34,515 people were arrested for suspected narcotics links, and over 34,000 weapons and $2.5 billion (street value) in drugs were seized over the previous year.[2] While part of the upbeat tone of the appraisal may represent actual "narco war" achievements, it must be tempered with the knowledge that Calderón has to maintain an optimistic political façade and continually sell his policies to the Mexican people. His *Partido Acción Nacional* (National Action Party [PAN]) may very likely lose the 2012 elections, including that for the presidency, to the more traditionally dominant *Partido Revolucionario Institucional* (Institutional Revolutionary Party [PRI]). Political expediency thus dictates that no communiqués will be issued that do not follow the "We are on the path of success" PAN party line.[3]

It would be expected, then, that the specter of the escalating Mexican cartel use of car bombs since mid-July 2010, for example, would be ignored in the *informe*. Within the executive summary of the report, specifically in the State of Law and Security section, this is what has happened — with no mention of the narco car bombs (*coche-bombas*) given at all.[4] Such bombings, the even more recent mass atrocity inflicted upon 72 migrants in Tamaulipas, and the multiple incidents of bodies hanging from bridges—sans genitals, index fingers, and heads in one instance, and arms in another—do not make for eloquent and polite Mexican political discourse.[5] Still, car bombings now represent a new reality for Mexico, part of the widening "narco nightmare" of violence, corruption, and criminal insurgency that is threatening the integrity and sovereignty of expanses of that country. Such bombings have amazed many researchers, not because they have taken place but because they took so long to finally come about. Car bombings in Mexico cannot be wished away or ignored and may now only be expected to continue, albeit hopefully in an intermittent and discriminant manner, into the foreseeable future.

As one co-author has noted, the July 15, 2010, Ciudad Juárez car bombing represents a firebreak in terms of "an apparently significant acceleration of tactics, techniques, and procedures (TTP)" for Mexican cartel violence.[6] Given the escalatory nature of these bombings to the conflict taking place in Mexico, and indeed the close proximity of them to the United States—some literally within miles of the border—they should be of at least some interest to local, state, and federal U.S. law enforcement and, ultimately, to the U.S. Army and other governmental institutions, which are increasingly providing support to Mexican federal agencies.

With this in mind, this Paper first seeks to provide an historical overview and analysis of cartel car bomb use in Mexico. In doing so, it provides context, insights, and lessons learned stemming from the Medellin and Cali cartel car bombing campaigns that plagued Colombia, primarily between 1988 and 1993. It then discusses the initial cartel car bombings that took place in Mexico in the early 1990s — car bombings that most researchers have overlooked — before highlighting indications and warnings (I&W) events identified in the years prior to the resumption of Mexican cartel car bombings in mid-2010. Contemporary car bombings in Mexico from mid-2010 through much of 2012 will then be discussed and analyzed.

Second, this Paper capitalizes on the historical overview and analysis provided from both the Mexican and earlier Colombian experiences in order to generate insights into future cartel car bombing potentials in Mexico. The identification of such potentials, in one sense, offers a glimpse into cartel "enemy intent" — a possible form of actionable strategic intelligence. The final section of this Paper offers conclusions stemming from the analysis provided and recommendations for the U.S. Army and other governmental institutions whose mission may somehow be impacted by the cartel car bombings now taking place in Mexico.

CAR BOMBINGS AND LESSONS LEARNED IN COLOMBIA

A review of the historical literature on car bomb use by the Colombian cartels suggests this is an understudied area and one beset with only fragmentary incident information.[7] Both the RAND Database of Worldwide Terrorism Incidents (RDWTI) and Global Terrorism Database (GTD) are almost useless as datasets concerning such car bombings.[8] A GTD search for Colombian (country) explosives/bombs/dynamite (weapons) and bombing/explosion (attacks) yielded 2,365 incidents between July 24, 1976, and December

29, 2008, with the vast majority minor in nature and conducted by the various indigenous guerilla groups.[9] Further, the sheer amount of bombings conducted by the Medellin cartel between 1988 and 1993, most of which do not exist in datasets nor distinguish between thrown/placed bombs and car bombs, make any form of quantitative analysis impossible. For instance, between mid-August and mid-December 1989 alone, it is estimated 205 bombings, mostly small in nature, were carried out.[10]

Still, even with this fragmentary information, some historical observations can be made concerning Colombian cartel bombing use. The first major car bombing took place outside the U.S. Embassy in Bogota in November 1984 and was meant as a "shot across the bow" to warn the Drug Enforcement Administration (DEA) to back off from its operations against Pablo Escobar and the other Medellin cartel leaders known as the "*Extraditables*."[11] The two competing drug cartels, based in Medellin and Cali respectively, did not engage in the sustained use of car bombs, however, until open war broke out between these two organizations in January 1988. Differing explanations are offered for the origins of the war. The first is based on the Cali cartel creating a Mexican route to the U.S. market, via an alliance with the Guadalajara cartel, which threatened Medellin cartel dominance. Another explanation viewed the war as starting over a power struggle between the cartels over the New York cocaine market.

A third reason was that the competing cartel bosses felt they were being disrespected by each other, neither side was willing to back down, and their honor had to take precedence over business.[12] Whatever the reason for the war, a Cali cartel car bomb, which targeted the family of Pablo Escobar in their luxury eighth story apartment in Medellin and permanently damaged his daughter's hearing, signaled open hostilities. The war raged between January 1988 and the death of Escobar in December 1993, with a lull while Escobar was sequestered in the palatial prison *La Cathedral* from June 1991 through July 1992. The Colombian government made a conscious decision during this cartel war to focus solely on the Medellin cartel, which was considered a far larger threat to the Colombian state and, by default, sided with the Cali cartel. After the demise of the Medellin cartel, the Colombian government, directly supported by the United States, would subsequently turn its attention to dismantling the Cali cartel. As a result, the Colombian government faced the direct wrath of the Medellin cartel for collusion with its enemies.

Table 1 provides an overview of some of the higher profile cartel car bombing incidents that took place during this war. Except for the initial car bombing that signaled open hostilities and may have been a calculated Cali cartel ploy to enrage Escobar, car bomb use was typically a Medellin cartel affair. Escobar had little concern for collateral damage resulting from these bombings and generally utilized good size payloads, with the December 1989 attack on the Colombian Administrative Department of Security (DAS) utilizing a massive 1,100-pound bomb that caused devastating destruction:

> 'The explosion,' reported the *New York Times*, 'was so powerful that it broke windows in a building across the street from the United States Embassy, *seven miles away*.' The largest car bomb ever detonated outside the Middle East left a 20-foot-crater in the street and devastated 23 city blocks. DAS commander, General Miguel Maza Marquez managed to survive the blast—which he described as a 'mini-atomic bomb'—in his steel plated ninth-floor office, but his secretary was

killed, along with 58 other people. An incredible 1000 workers, residents, and pedestrians were injured (250 seriously), and at least 1500 homes and office buildings suffered significant damage. The toll might have been even more catastrophic had police not defused a second car bomb placed in front of judicial offices.[13]

Date	City	Perpetrator/Type	Fatalities/ Injured	Target
January 13, 1988	Medellin	Cali Cartel; Car bomb	2/1[a]	Pablo Escobar's Home/Luxury 8th Story Apartment
~ August 1988	Cali	Medellin Cartel; Renault with 200 lb bomb	7/24[a]	La Rebaja Drug Store (Cali Cartel owned)
May 25, 1989	Bogota	Medellin Cartel	6/50[a]	Miguel Maza (Head of DAS)
December 6, 1989	Medellin	Medellin Cartel; Car with 1,100 lbs of dynamite	58/1000[a,d]	DAS Headquarters
March 1990	Cali, Bogota, Medellin	Medellin Cartel; Multiple car bombs detonated simultaneously	26/200[a]	Unknown
April 11, 1990	Itagui	Medellin Cartel; Suspected car bomb	16/109[c]	Truck Carrying Police Anti-Terrorism Unit
December 2, 1992	Medellin	Medellin Cartel; Huge car bomb	10/3[b]	Police by Stadium
January 30, 1993	Bogota	Medellin Cartel; Car with 220 lbs of dynamite	21/70[b]	Civilians in Bookstore
April 15, 1993	Bogota	Medellin Cartel; Car with +300 lbs of dynamite	11/200[b]	Civilians in busy Intersection/ Shopping Center

Sources: Ron Chepesiuk, *Drug Lords: The Rise and the Fall of the Cali Cartel*[a]; Mark Bowden, *Killing Pablo*[b]; *Global Terrorism Database*[c] and newspaper archives.[d]

Table 1. Selected Medellin and Cali Cartel Car Bomb Use in Colombia.

While some of the car bombs were used in an insurgency role that targeted police in 1989, 1990, and 1992, the final car bombs used in 1993 were used in a terrorism role against civilian targets when Escobar was on the run and increasingly feared for his life. Dynamite was the only named explosive used in any of the car bombings with timer detonators (and in one instance a potential lighted fuse) mentioned in the incident accounts.

The strife between the Medellin and Cali cartels extended beyond Colombia. According to Ron Chepesiuk:

> The war spread to the United States, and, in the last week of August [1988], the media reported on several dozen bombings in New York City and in Miami.[14]

While professional killers were indeed being deployed to these cities from Colombia — the Cali cartel brought in more than 10^{15} — and the death toll for both Medellin and Cali cartel operatives and associates in these cities may have numbered well into the dozens, these bombing incidents cannot be substantiated. The Chepesiuk quote is referenced to a *New York Times* article that makes no mention of actual bombings taking place.[16] RDWTI, GTD, and city news searches yielded no incidents of such bombings or incendiary attacks.[17] This is not surprising since *sicarios* (assassins) typically killed using small arms, with the Mac-10 (and lighter Mac-11 variant) machine pistol then highly favored. Still, both cartels easily had the resources to deploy bomb makers to the United States if desired, and, if nothing else, ad hoc Molotov cocktail attacks would have been relatively simple for the *sicarios* to utilize against those in opposing safe houses.[18] Prior to the 1988 hostilities, Medellin cartel boss Griselda "Black Widow" Blanco of Miami, FL, ordered numerous killings during the 1979-84 period. Her contract killer, Jorge "Rivi" Ayala, stated in a prison interview for the documentary *Cocaine Cowboys* that he even dynamited a house in an attempt to kill an opposing cartel rival.[19] Still, no reference to actual car bomb use in the United States by either the Medellin or Cali cartel has been found anywhere in the scholarly literature or in media reports.[20]

The lessons learned from Colombian cartel car bomb use appear to be twofold. First, car bombs were not only used in Colombia as a warning to others but also in an anti-personnel role to kill government agents, rival traffickers, and civilians; and in an anti-infrastructure role to damage and destroy public, commercial, and private facilities and buildings. Cali cartel use of car bombs was more highly discriminate in its application and initially focused on targeting the family of Pablo Escobar, the leader of the rival Medellin cartel. Later, in 1993, according to Mike Davis, the Cali cartel capitalized on public anger and detonated two additional car bombs in front of apartment buildings in which Escobar's immediate and extended family members were residing.[21] This is in line with the second phase cartel attributes identified for Cali, based on its propensity to emphasize corruption and symbolic violence over indiscriminate and mass killing.[22] The Medellin cartel, on the other hand, actively engaged in mass killing, especially later on, primarily directed at vestiges of the Colombian state and its citizenry. Further, it also actively targeted elements of the Cali cartel with little concern for collateral damage inflicted upon others. This pattern of car bomb use is in line with the designation of the Medellin cartel as a first phase "aggressive competitor" habituated to extreme violence and, ultimately, a major reason for its eventual downfall in late 1993.[23] It should be noted that car bomb use by both cartels in Colombia did not exist in a vacuum and were interspersed with the more frequent use of thrown and placed bombs, kidnappings, and assassinations, and street level firefights.[24]

Second, while the Medellin and Cali narco-war of 1988 in Colombia spread to some of the key distribution cities in the United States, the level of violence remained relatively restrained and never approached the blatant violence witnessed during the much earlier July 1979 Dadeland Mall massacre.[25] In fact, while assassinations and intercartel killings were common and small scale bombings may have been relatively rare occurrences, no record of any cartel car bombings taking place in the United States have been identified. Some sort of psychological "firebreak" existed that even the more feral operatives of the Medellin cartel respected, thus deterring car bomb use on U.S. soil. Quite possibly, the specter of overwhelming U.S. law enforcement response locally, and the eventual blowback in Colombia at the highest governmental levels against the cartels, made such car bombings and the ensuing public and media spectacle that it would create a politically toxic option for someone even as violent as Pablo Escobar.

EARLY CAR BOMBINGS IN MEXICO

Bombs have been utilized in Mexico for politically related terrorist purposes, often targeted at U.S. and other interests, since the early 1970s. In February 1974, seven such devices damaged Pepsi Cola and Union

Carbide plants in Guadalajara and other companies in Oaxaca. The perpetrators were never identified.[26] A diverse mixture of leftist, Indian rebel, and anarchist bombings, with groups such as the 23rd of September Communist League, Zapatista Army, and Armed Revolutionary Front of the People (FARP) claiming responsibility, have persisted into the 2000s. These bombings have taken place both in urban locales, such as Acapulco and Mexico City, and in the countryside, for example, against pipelines in the states of Guanajuato and Querétaro.[27]

The majority of these bombings utilized small devices that were either placed or thrown. Three car bomb or vehicle borne improvised explosive device (VBIED) incidents, however, did take place.[28] The first incident, which even predates the 1974 spree of bombings, took place in July 1972. According to the RAND Database of Worldwide Terrorism Incidents:

> A panel truck containing plastic cans filled with gasoline to which were attached dynamite caps exploded in front of the U.S. consulate general in Monterey, destroying the truck but causing no damage to the consulate general.[29]

The terrorist group involved with the incident was not discovered. The second incident, which represents a quasi-car bomb, took place in November 1974, and targeted Fernando Lopez Muino, the Cuban ambassador to Mexico.[30] A bomb was placed in his car by anti-Castro Cubans and detonated; however, the ambassador did not sustain any injuries. The last incident took place in 1986 in Mexico City. According to the RDWTI:

A caller tipped off police about a bomb in a car parked in front of the U.S. Embassy in Mexico City. The sophisticated device was defused 15 minutes before it was set to go off. The Simon Bolivar Anti-Imperialist Commando claimed responsibility for the action, linking it to the U.S. air strike in Libya.[31]

The earliest Mexican drug cartel related car bombing took place 20 years after the first politically related terrorist car bomb incident. It can be traced back to a car bomb detonated outside of a house used by "El Chapo" Guzmán, a head of the Sinaloa cartel in Culiacán in 1992, shortly after the Arellano Felix brothers (Tijuana cartel) put a bounty on his head. El Chapo and his bodyguards were not at the residence, and no one was injured from the bombing.[32] The next identifiable cartel related car bombing took place at a hotel in Guadalajara in June 1994. A newspaper account of the incident summarized it as follows:

> A car packed with powerful explosives blew up outside a luxury hotel Saturday, killing at least five people and wounding 15. Police sources said the bombing may be linked to Guadalajara's drug gangs.
>
> The Camino Real Hotel was evacuated after the early morning explosion, which occurred as 300 guests were winding up a debutante ball for a 15-year-old-girl. Investigators at the scene, speaking on condition of anonymity, said the girl's family is known to have ties to drug traffickers.
>
> The Mexico City newspaper Universal reported that police said members of the family of Rafael Caro Quintero, allegedly one of Mexico's most powerful drug traffickers, were attending the party inside the hotel.

. . . Police and state officials said the automobile was packed with 10-22 pounds of plastic explosives and may have been detonated by remote control. Enrique Hoyos Medina, an expert at the state attorney general's office, said the explosives were a commercial type sold mainly to mining companies.[33]

The only other reference to cartel related car bombings during the 1990s is one mentioned by Barnard Thompson, a long-time private security specialist in Mexico and Latin America and editor of *MexiData. info,* who states:

With respect to the car bombing count, the fact is since 1992 there have been at least five 'vehicle borne improvised explosive devices' that exploded, three of which appeared to be part of cartel infighting that unsuccessfully targeted Ismael 'El Mayo' Zambada García, drug kingpin of the Sinaloa Cartel. The others, one in Chiapas and another in Acapulco, Guerrero, against nearby quasi-government and military installations, were thought to be by small guerilla groups for supposed social causes.[34]

These car bombings against El Chapo Guzmán, the family of "El Numero Uno" Caro (the cartel leader had been incarcerated in April 1985), and El Mayo Zambada resulted from the dissolution of the Guadalajara cartel and the early wars between the Sinaloa and Tijuana factions. Given the excessive and indiscriminate violence utilized by the Arellano Felix brothers, including the use of San Diego based Logan Heights gang assassins who mistakenly killed Cardinal Posadas Ocampo at Guadalajara International Airport in May 1993,[35] it is highly likely that this early phase of cartel car bombings was carried out solely by the Tijuana cartel. If this is the case, it would be testament to the Sinaloa cartel's better strategic appreciation of the consequences of its actions and unwillingness to blindly engage in tit-for-tat retaliatory violence with its cartel competitors.

RECENT INDICATIONS AND WARNINGS FOR RESUMED CAR BOMB USE IN MEXICO

With a deescalation of cartel violence between the Tijuana and Sinaloa cartels in the early 1990s, the use of car bombs ceased for over 15 years. Some sort of crude or mock car bomb—based on a container of gasoline, a false antenna, and cell phone (with either an inert or no detonator)—was then reported in August 2005. It had been placed in a stolen vehicle that was parked at a Guadalajara shopping center for 3 days and discovered by a security guard.[36] Whether this device was tied to Mexican cartel violence is unknown. Following the December 2006 Calderón offensive against the cartels and narco gangs in Mexico, violence levels once again increased. Along with this increase in violence, attempted and actual bombings using grenades and improvised explosive devices (IEDs), already beginning to take place, increased in frequency. Suspected grenade attacks in April and August 2006 were targeted against a "... busy restaurant in the Pacific coast town of Petatlán, Mexico ..." and against "... the offices of two newspapers, Por Esto and Quequi Quintana Roo, in Cancun, Mexico. . ."[37] In June 2007:

> ... police deactivated two bombs in two south Mexico City subway stations after being tipped off. Both bombs were accompanied by packages related to drug traffickers.[38]

More bombings then took place, including the pre-denotation of a bomb two blocks from Mexico City's police headquarters in February 2008 — the dead bomber belonging to the Tepito drug gang had suspected links to the Sinaloa cartel and an operative known as "El Patron."[39] Also, the infamous Los Zetas linked fragmentation grenades attack, killing eight and injuring 101, on a crowd of people celebrating Mexican Independence Day in Morelia, Michoacán, was carried out in September 2008.[40] During this same period in July 2008, an I&W event took place related to the start of a new cycle of car bomb use:

> Mexican drug traffickers have built make shift car bombs to attack police, troops and rival smugglers as the country's drug war turns increasingly violent, police said.
>
> Soldiers found two car bombs in a safe house in the city of Culiacan in western Mexico on Monday. One car was packed with cans of gasoline and another stuffed with canisters of gas, police said.
>
> Both devices were wired to be detonated by cell phones, said a police official in Culiacan, capital of Sinaloa state, which is home to one of Mexico's biggest trafficking cartels.[41]

Speculation exists that the car bombs may have belonged to a Sinaloa faction controlled by Joaquin "Shorty" Guzmán, who broke off from other local drug lords and is no longer allied to them.[42] Regardless of the origins of these devices, their existence, the increasing patterns of violence in the Mexican drug wars, and the proliferation of small IED and grenade incidents (72 grenade attacks estimated in 2009 alone)[43] suggest car bomb use would once again resume in

Mexico. This time around, however, their use may not be confined to only one cartel and could conceivably follow the more brutal and less discriminate patterns of car bombings that were conducted in Colombia by the Medellin cartel beginning in the mid-1980s.

CONTEMPORARY CAR BOMBINGS IN MEXICO

Recognition that Mexican cartel violence had embraced the car bomb followed the July 15, 2010, attack on Federal police in embattled Ciudad Juárez. In that incident, a primitive IED—not the fully integrated VBIED variant found in Iraq and the AfPak (Afghanistan-Pakistan) theaters—was secreted inside a car. The ambush attack directly targeted the police and can be considered a classic TTP of insurgents. The attack was widely heralded as the drug war's first car bombing, which historically we know is not the case, and spurred a semantic debate over the difference between "car bombs" and "bombs in cars."

Four persons were killed in this well-planned, "bait and wait" trap near a Federal police facility. The attack was the first documented use of a car bomb by drug traffickers or their affiliated gangs since the start of Mexico's countercartel offensive by Calderón in 2006. Clearly, the use of bombs (ranging from simple IEDs to the more complex large vehicle bomb [LVB], erstwhile known as a VBIED) portends to dramatically alter the nature of Mexico's drug wars.

Until this assault, cartels and their paramilitary gangsters largely relied on small arms, limited use of grenades, and symbolic beheadings to neutralize competing cartel and government security forces. While police in Sinaloa found improvised gas canister car bombs cached for potential use in July 2008, participants in the drug war relied upon barbaric beheadings, bold small arms attacks (active shootings), and the occasional grenade or combined small arms-grenade attack to wage their battles. While all these means are a challenge to police, the potential specter of urban car bombings — with their attendant casualty generating capacity — poses a threat potential similar to the "conventional" insurgencies of Iraq and Afghanistan. After the July 15 car bombing, which is believed to have been conducted by La Línea, a *narcomensaje* or message left at the scene claimed the Juárez cartel was responsible for the car bombing and threatened further attacks. "We still have car bombs," claimed the alleged warning.[44]

According to Associated Press reports:

> . . . the La Linea drug gang — the same group blamed for the killing of a U.S. consulate employee and her husband in March 2010 — lured federal officers and paramedics to the site of a car bomb by dressing a bound, wounded man in a police uniform and calling in a false report of an officer shot. . . . The gang then exploded a car holding as much as 22 pounds (10 kilograms) of explosives, killing the decoy, a rescue worker, and a federal officer.[45]

While the Juárez platform was a simple car bomb, not a fully evolved VBIED, the debate over terminology rages. VBIED is a jargon-laden term preferred by military and security analysts familiar with U.S. counterinsurgency efforts in Iraq and Afghanistan. Some observers, notably STRATFOR, make it a point to distinguish between the fully evolved variant and their simple cousins.[46] The sophistication or operational effectiveness of the device is only one element of the attack and should not be overconflated with the TTP or delivery platform. Remember, "Buda's Wagon" (the first modern "car" bomb) detonated in September 1920 by the corner of Wall and Broad Streets in New York City was not sophisticated in terms of the devices encountered in Colombia, Iraq, or the AfPak theaters either, but it was still a car bomb.[47]

The Ciudad Juárez device was likely a transitional weapon. It is plausible that cartel bomb makers were experimenting and importing TTP from other conflicts to exploit on their own battleground. Indeed, after the Juárez attack, at least 18 car bomb incidents have been recorded in Mexico. Table 2 documents these attacks, as well as the initial Juárez incident and a precursor incident in Culiacán 2 years prior.[48] As Table 2 demonstrates, the recent use of car bombs as a tactic of confrontation is now more prevalent than widely recognized. Use of the tactic starts with one precursor interdiction in 2008, followed by no use in 2009. In 2010, the year of the July 15 sentinel attack in Ciudad Juárez, five incidents were recorded. In 2011, a total of eight incidents were documented. One incident each occurred in Sinaloa and Hidalgo, two incidents in Ciudad Juárez, three incidents in Nuevo León, and four in Ciudad Victoria (Tamaulipas). While the offending actors are not definitively known, both Tamaulipas and Nuevo León are areas contested by the Zetas and Gulf cartels. A brief overview of these incidents follows. The first incident recorded after the July 15 attack targeted the headquarters of the Tamaulipas State Public Safety agency. A car bomb rocked the complex in Ciudad Victoria on August 5, 2010. No one was hurt, but two police cars were damaged.[49] On August 27, a car bomb exploded outside the offices of *Televisa* in Ciudad Victoria, causing damage and interrupting the station's broadcast, however, no one was injured.[50]

Date	City	Perpetrator/Type	Fatalities/Injuries	Target
July 14, 2008	Culiacán, Sinaloa	Unknown, possibly Sinaloa cartel; 2 car bombs with gas canisters captured	0/0	Likely intended to target police
July 15, 2010	Ciudad Juárez, Chihuahua	La Línea; car bomb	4/0	Police on foot responding to call; ambush
August 5, 2010	Ciudad Victoria, Tamaulipas	Unknown; car bomb	0/0	Headquarters building; state police
August 27, 2010	Ciudad Victoria, Tamaulipas	Unknown; car bomb	0/0	Televisa building
September 10, 2010	Ciudad Juárez, Chihuahua	Unknown; car bomb	Interdicted	Police on foot responding to call; ambush attempt
September 2010	Guadalajara, Jalisco	Unknown; car bomb	Interdicted	Unknown
January 18, 2011	Linares, Nuevo León	Unknown; 2 car bombs	0/3	Police
January 22, 2011	Tula-Tepeji, Hidalgo	Zetas; car bomb	1/3	Police
March 15, 2011	Ciudad Victoria, Tamaulipas	Unknown; car bomb	0/5	Police station (proximate to day care center)
September 12, 2011	Ciudad Juárez, Chihuahua	Unknown; car bomb	0/0	Day care center; police (ambush attempt)
September 16, 2011	Ciudad Victoria, Tamaulipas	Unknown; car bomb	0/0	Unknown, possibly police
October 10, 2011	Monterrey, Nuevo León	Zetas assumed; car bomb	0/0	Military patrol (Vehicular)
December 18, 2011	Zuazua, Nuevo León	Unknown; car bomb	0/3	Police station
January 10, 2012	Ciudad Victoria, Tamaulipas	Unknown; car bomb	Interdicted	Police station
March 19, 2012	Ciudad Victoria, Tamaulipas	Unknown; car bomb	0/0	Expreso newspaper building
April 24, 2012	Nuevo Laredo, Tamaulipas	Sinaloa assumed; car bomb	0/0	Headquarters building; police
May 24, 2012	Nuevo Laredo, Tamaulipas	Zetas assumed; car bomb	0/10	Barracks at hotel; police
June 6, 2012	Ciudad Victoria, Tamaulipas	Unknown; 2 car bombs (arson)	0/0	Car dealership

**Table 2. Contemporary Car Bomb (*coche-bomba*)
Incidents in Mexico.**

June 29, 2012	Nuevo Laredo, Tamaulipas	Unkown; car bomb	0/7	City Hall; Municipal Government
July 3, 2012	Ciudad Victoria, Tamaulipas	Unknown; car bomb	2/7	Private Residence; Chief Security Officer
July 31, 2012	Culiacán, Sinaloa	Unknown; car bomb	0/0	Gas Station

Sources: English and Spanish language media reports

Table 2. Contemporary Car Bomb (*coche-bomba*) Incidents in Mexico. (cont.)

Then, in September 2010, two incidents took place. One, on September 10, took place in Ciudad Juárez and involved another ambush in which an explosive device was placed in a car next to a car containing a dead body, which had been reported to the local police. The device, which contained 16 kilograms of the explosive Tovex, apparently failed to detonate and was rendered safe by a Mexican military ordnance team. The other incident took place in Guadalajara sometime in September and was composed of a liquor bottle filled with explosives placed inside a car. The device was recovered prior to its detonation and was unique because of the Futaba radio-contoller that was wired to it. Such controllers, used for model aircraft, can be traced back to Medellin cartel VBIEDs deployed in Colombia 2 decades ago.[51]

In 2011, we start to see the acceleration of the car bomb TTP. In January, two car bombs were deployed in Linares, Nuevo León. No one was injured in the first attack, but three people were wounded in the second. Both incidents targeted police. On January 22, Hidalgo was brought into the equation, with the Zetas attacking the police in a bombing that killed one police officer and injured three. On March 15, five persons were wounded when a parked car bomb detonated outside a police station in Ciudad Victoria. The police station was situated next to a child-care center. On September 12, police disarmed a car bomb in the parking lot of a day care center. It is suspected that the device was meant to detonate when police arrived, but it was rendered safe. Later that month, on September 16 in Ciudad Victoria, a car bomb was detonated in the Colonia 7 de Noviembre in Ciudad Victoria, but no casualties were reported. In October, a Mexican army patrol was targeted in a car bomb ambush, but no injuries resulted. Finally, on December 18, 2011, a car bomb exploded outside a police station in Zuazua, Nuevo León, injuring three.[52]

The growing sophistication of Mexican cartel car bombs can be better understood by looking at an initial tactical analysis of the early morning October 20, 2011, car bomb ambush directed against a Mexican military patrol on Avenida Revolucion in Monterrey:

> . . . A cell phone detonated improvised explosive device (IED) placed inside the trunk of a small sedan is the most plausible — making it a VBIED (vehicle borne IED) — method of attack. The explosive type utilized is unknown but C-4 is quite probable; *these assumptions have not been confirmed forensically and therefore are only speculative*. A cartel vehicle was used as bait to bring a mounted Mexican Army patrol into the prepared kill zone. The VBIED was detonated prematurely with no soldiers or civilians injured in the ambush. Scenario 1: The VBIED was meant to be utilized in an efficient anti-vehicular/anti-personnel role to produce maximum Mexican military causalities. The ambush was unsuccessful due to the premature VBIED detonation and/or the explosive yield/dynamics utilized (small

yield/non-directional). Scenario 2: The VBIED was utilized symbolically (as a warning) to the Mexican military to cease/limit their operations in Monterrey... No matter the accuracy of either scenario, this incident represents the first recorded use of a VBIED against a mounted Mexican Army patrol and a further escalation of VBIED tactical evolution taking place in the criminal insurgencies in Mexico. . . .[53]

Additional attacks were threatened in December, with car bombings resuming 1 month later in January 2012, with eight total incidents taking place through July. In Ciudad Victoria, Tamaulipas, the state police station was targeted with a car containing explosives in the trunk parked next to it. The car had been left next to the police station on the night of January 9, had luckily failed to detonate, and was disarmed by Mexican Federal police bomb disposal experts early the next morning.[54] Then, on March 19, a car bomb was used to target the *Expreso* newspaper in Ciudad Victoria, Tamaulipas. The device exploded at 8:15 p.m. on Monday on Avenida Los Almendros next to the newspaper building. No casualties resulted from the blast, but a couple of nearby vehicles and the building did suffer some property damage, and the newspaper website was down the next morning.[55]

On April 24, a car bomb was detonated in front of the building housing the attorney general of Tamaulipas and various state and municipal police agencies in Nuevo Laredo. The low yield device, suspected of belonging to the Sinaloa cartel, was set off at 8:00 a.m. on Tuesday morning. Pictures of the incident show minor fragmentation damage to a guard post, limiting perimeter access, and to a section of the building. Minor window breakage, the partial destruction of the actual pickup truck that contained the device, and a nearby patrol car, are also evident. No casualties resulted from the detonation, however, an ensuing firefight between Mexican soldiers and armed cartel gunmen was reported to have taken place right after the bombing.[56]

The next bombing also took place in Nuevo Laredo, Tamaulipas — this time on May 24, 2012. The attack came at 5:30 a.m. on Thursday morning and was initiated by the Zetas against state police, who were barracked at the Hotel Santa Cecilia. Eight law enforcement officers and two civilians were wounded in what turned out to be a combined arms attack that began with gunfire directed against the hotel, followed by the detontation of a car bomb. Damage to the façade of an "L" shaped corner of a small motel with parking next to the rooms was evident in photos of the incident. Three of the officers sustained third-degree burns, which suggests that the initial gunfire drew them into the killing zone right outside of their rooms with the bomb placed in a pickup truck parked next to them. A police car and a privately owned car were also damaged from the detonation.[57]

A minor car bombing incident then took place in Ciudad Victoria, Tamaulipas, on Wednesday, June 6, 2012, at a Renualt and Volkswagen car dealership. Two vehicles were engulfed in flames by means of grenades or some other explosive device, which set their gas tanks on fire. Rather than a targeted attack against law enforcement or military personnel, this incident appears to simply represent arson for extortion purposes being directed at the car dealership by either the Zetas or the Gulf/Sinaloa cartels.[58] The city hall in Nuevo Laredo was then targeted by a bomb placed in a Ford Ranger pickup on Friday, June 29, 2012. The detonation of the device took place at 11:00

a.m. in the morning, injured seven people, and caused damage to 11 nearby vehicles, the side of the city hall, and local businesses. The blast was large enough for a plume of smoke to be seen from the U.S. side of the border. Of note is that the pickup was parked next to the mayor's parking spot, and the incident took place 48 hours prior to the national presidential elections in Mexico.[59]

On Tuesday, July 3, 2012, a car bomb was detonated in Ciudad Victoria in front of the private residence of the top security official in the state of Tamaulipas a few days after the national elections. The blast killed two police officers and wounded seven police officers and civilians. Damage to nearby vehicles was evident in an incident photo. The car bomb was said to be cell phone activated and was parked near the security barrier on the street just outside the official's residence.[60] Finally, on Tuesday, July 31, 2012, a bomb in a stolen car was detonated at a gas station in Culiacán, Sinaloa. No one was injured in the incident, and several homemade bombs were recovered from the car wreckage. No other information was provided in the news report.[61]

ANALYSIS AND FUTURE CAR BOMBING POTENTIALS IN MEXICO AND THE UNITED STATES

The present round of cartel car bomb deployment since July 2008 has been gradually increasing albeit in a sporadic and haphazard manner, with about 20 incidents now identified. It has been primarily directed at Mexican law enforcement and military personnel and officials. Secondary deployment against media and business interests has also been identified — although it is unclear if the nonmedia business establishments were always the intended targets, and whether incendiary attacks via hand grenade detonation of car fuel tanks, rather than actual explosives, were TTP utilized.[62] Still, these recent cartel deployment patterns in Mexico suggest the following reasons for car bomb use have taken place. It is expected that these patterns will continue into the near future:

1. Primary Use Reasons
   - Threats and Warnings
   - Psychological Warfare/Terrorism
2. Secondary Use Reasons
   - Diversion Creation
   - Anti-personnel Targeting
   - Anti-vehicular/Anti-materiel Targeting

To date, no direct evidence exists to suggest that car bombs have been used in intercartel engagements. Instead, the cartels have relied upon direct ambushes and armed assaults to combat each other, but this could change if a specific cartel faces an existential threat from another cartel (or the state). Precedent for a reversion to intercartel car bomb deployment can be drawn to the Arellano Felix and Sinaloa conflict in the early 1990s. Further, at varying points in the narco-conflict, it is likely that cartels will have different use trajectories ranging from nondeployment to some of the deployment patterns described previously. Cartels either confirmed or alleged to have attempted or conducted car bombings are the Tijuana cartel (1990s only), the Juárez cartel, the Gulf cartel, Los Zetas, and even the Sinaloa cartel—which is not normally thought to use such weapons:

The use of car bombs is a strategy used primarily by the Sinaloa cartel, which has allied with the Gulf Cartel to fight the Zetas, said a Mexican federal law enforcement official who asked not to be named for security reasons.

'The Zetas typically use grenades, but the Sinaloans are a little more sophisticated when it comes to that and used explosives,' the official said in Spanish. 'Car bombs have been employed in Nuevo Laredo, Monterrey, Victoria and the Tamaulipas coast city of Tampico, which are contested cities,' the official said. 'Depending on where those groups are fighting, that's where you could see' the bombs.[63]

Still, even with the statement provided by the Mexican official, intercartel engagements using car bombs cannot be substantiated—at best, they may be targeting each other's co-opted law enforcement proxies.

Of further note is a lack of car bomb deployment allegations directed against La Familia Michoacana and Los Caballeros Templarios (The Knights Templar). While these groups—both the initial and the successor organization—have utilized IEDs, fragmentation grenades, and even heavier infantry weapons such as rocket propelled grenades (RPGs), no attempted use of car bombs have been identified to date. This is significant because the spirituality of Los Caballeros Templarios appears increasingly conducive to martyrdom potentials—derived from retro-Christian "blood of the lamb" symbolism—which, if combined with the VBIED TTP, results in Mexican cartel suicide car bomber potentials.

Also, no evidence of present Mexican cartel car bomb deployment for anti-infrastructure purposes exists such as that undertaken in Colombia by the Medellin and Cali cartels. Fred Burton, Chief Security Officer of STRATFOR, provided a well-articulated analysis in a video report on this subject. His analysis suggests that while the "capability" to deploy large scale car bombs against public buildings presently exists, the "intent" to undertake such attacks by the Mexican cartels does not.[64] One example of the capability possessed by the cartels is illustrated by the February 2009 raid upon an explosives magazine operated by a company from Texas doing business in Durango, Mexico:

> Two white Suburban-type SUV's rolled up and 15 to 20 masked men stepped out bearing automatic rifles. 'The security guards were ordered at gunpoint to open the magazine, and the gunmen made off with a large quantity of Tovex brand explosives and electric detonators,' reads a report by the United States Bomb Data Center obtained by GlobalPost. . . .
>
> . . . The report states that 267.75 pounds or 900 cartridges of the explosives as well as 230 electric detonators were taken. . . .[65]

That amount of explosive material is about 10 times the yield of the low yield car bombs deployed by the cartels to date. Even more explosives, "412 chubs (plastic sleeves) of hydrogel commercial explosives" were seized from the cartels along with "36 electric detonators and more than 11 meters of detonation cord" in Matamoros, Tamaulipas, in April 2011.[66]

It is thought by Burton and others that the cartels are not deploying larger yield car bombs because of the immense jumping of a "firebreak" such an escalatory deployment would represent. Crossing it would not only potentially trigger public outrage, but also possibly further escalate the state crackdown on the perpetrator cartel involved with using such a large

VBIED—it might even trigger increased U.S. governmental support to Mexico over what would be considered a watershed event. Of note, however, is the possible recent use of hand grenade detonation of car fuel tanks for arson purposes. This would represent a more subtle form of anti-infrastructure attack that would limit the media effect if done after hours to an establishment containing few to no employees.

Forecasting mid- and long-term cartel car bomb deployment patterns is more problematic. Although the devices employed to date are relatively crude and have yet to yield a high casualty count, over the last few years, they have increasingly been used as a tool of confrontation. As the conflict matures, it is plausible that the use and quality (tactical lethality) of car bombs will increase as a similar escalation has been seen in other conflicts.[67]

Mexico's criminal insurgencies appear to be escalating not only with the use of car bombs, but other explosives including hand grenades (many apparently stolen from Central American military arsenals) are also being employed. Clearly, grenades are not new in the Mexican narco-war, with thousands being seized from the gangs and cartels during the Calderón presidency.[68] In fact, in one well-known incident on September 15, 2008, *sicarios* tossed grenades into a crowd celebrating Mexico's independence in Morelia, Michoacán, killing eight people and wounding more than 100.

Grenades have also been used in assaults on police convoys and public officials, foreshadowing future car bomb potentials. Additionally, in the roughly 3 1/2-year period preceding July 2010, the Mexican attorney general's office made public the fact that 101 grenade attacks against government buildings had taken place.[69]

Further concerns over increases in the tactical lethality of cartel weaponry can be witnessed by the appearance of more sophisticated systems such as claymore mines, mortar shells, and various forms of anti-tank munitions such as Russian RPGs and older U.S. LAWs.[70] All of these weapons have the potential to be incorporated into future cartel VBIED systems to boost their effectiveness and/or be used in tandem with those systems in a combined arms manner.

So, while a firebreak on cartel car bomb use for anti-infrastructure purposes presently exists, it cannot be considered sacrosanct. Wounded cartels, like wild animals, may be willing to resort to drastic measures (or at least threaten to undertake them) if they feel cornered. This was evident with the Juárez cartel (aka the Vicente Carrillo Fuentes organization) following their July 2010 use of a car bomb ambush against responding police:

> La Linea threatened to employ a far larger IED (100 kilograms, or 220 pounds) if the FBI and the U.S. Drug Enforcement Administration (DEA) did not investigate the head of Chihuahua State Police intelligence, whom the VCF claimed was working for the Sinaloa Federation.[71]

The U.S. Government then went on to recognize the seriouness of cartel VBIED potentials in Mexico and deployed protective barriers at the U.S. Consulate in Monterrey on April 5, 2011.[72] With this in mind, steady state, slowly increasing, and quickly increasing car bomb use potentials in Mexico exists. The prognosis for decreasing car bomb deployment currently appears unlikely—especially for analysts who have watched the death toll steadily rise in Mexico from the thousands to the low tens-of-thousands to likely now over 80,000 individuals during the 6-year Calderón administration.[73]

These use trajectories include a continuation of the **intermittent and targeted (discrete violence) with low yields** currently evident. The next level up is deployment patterns seen moving on to a mid-range potential where cartels employ car bombs in **occasional and targeted high yield attacks** (targeting police military and government facilities with more lethal variants of current platforms). A final and dire potential is **frequent and indiscriminate use of car bombs** (to kill lots of people); this represents the worst case — an unlikely potential scenario and representative of what took place back in Colombia decades ago. Thus far, car bombs have been used mainly in symbolic attacks against police — in fact, the total of all the dead and wounded from all cartel car bombs detonated to date in Mexico have not, as of yet, surpassed the casualties from the singular 2008 Morelia grenade attack. At best, these contemporary attacks were likely intended to dissuade and disrupt enforcement actions by police and military forces (or in the case of the *Televisa* and *Expreso* attacks, to shape reportage of cartel action). This use is largely symbolic violence with an instrumental purpose. Crude, small yield devices suffice to make the statement. Should the cartels seek to engage in higher levels of direct confrontation with the state (including police and military forces), they may seek to use more sophisticated or higher yield devices. Similar potentials have to at least be considered should the cartels opt to use car bombs as instruments of retaliation for arrests by the Mexican government or against other cartels — at that point, the potentials for Colombian level car bombing casualties in the hundreds may exist.

The specter of car bombings in Mexico's drug war also raises concerns across the border in the United States. These concerns include fear that the extreme violence of Mexico's criminal insurgency could spill over into the United States. Beheadings, mass executions, the use of improvised armored vehicles (narco-tanks), social cleansing, and internally displaced persons suggest a macabre conflict has already emerged in Mexico.[74] In fact, since about 2006, beheadings have gone from a relatively unheard of event to more than 1,300 of them now being documented in the conflict between the gangs, cartels, and the Mexican state.[75]

Amplified by political concerns about illegal migration, some even see an alien horde ready to cross the Rio Grande, wreaking havoc throughout the United States, where Mexican cartels now operate in well over 1,000 cities.[76] Since some cartels have threatened U.S. law enforcement officials—even at times placing bounties for their killing[77]—a concern is that cartels will ambush American police, potentially with car bombs used in an anti-personnel and/or anti-vehicular role. In one incident, a street gang member actually threw a fragmentation grenade into a Pharr, Texas, bar containing off duty officers in January 2009.[78] Precedent for such an ambush scenario can be drawn to a June 2008 Phoenix, AZ, incident in which a cartel kill-team was dressed in local special weapons attack team (SWAT) gear (an older uniform type) and, after a successful assassination of a local drug dealer, attempted to draw a responding police officer into an ambush.[79]

Other scenarios include attacks on U.S. diplomatic personnel and consulates in Mexico, as well as attacks on border infrastructure or even U.S. Army posts and guard armories. However, the use of car bombs, at least on U.S. soil and directed at U.S. governmental personnel operating in Mexico, is presently far from a likely potential.[80] Organized crime groups (including the Mexican cartels) are more likely to seek to evade or corrupt and co-opt state actors than to confront the state, especially as one as strong as the United States.[81] Cartel behavior in Mexico, as we have seen, is an entirely different matter, however, and becomes more and more emboldened with success as their impunity grows. This concern exists especially in towns, cities, and regions that fall under their de facto politicial control—many of which just happen to reside close to the U.S. border—because it may result in "hybrid" cartel behavior in some sovereign U.S. territory, which is less brazen than that found in Mexico but bolder than traditionally encountered in the United States.[82]

If cartel car bombs were to be eventually deployed on U.S. soil or against U.S. personnel and facilities in Mexico such as our consulates, we could expect that a pattern of I&W would be evident prior to such an attack or attacks.[83] In that case, I&W would be drawn from precursor events such as grenade and IED attacks (or attempted attacks) on our personnel and facilities and on evolving cartel car bomb deployment patterns in Mexico, especially concerning increases in tactical lethality and a shift toward anti-infrastructure targeting.

CONCLUSIONS AND RECOMMENDATIONS

Essentially, the problem faced by both Mexican military and police agencies and U.S. police agencies is that combating potential high intensity/criminal insurgency attacks employing car bombs demands real-time intelligence support and superb tactical and operational command, control, and communications, all of which require new doctrine, training, and equipment. Basically, we are seeing the need to develop "intra-conflict" policing capacity. Such a capacity requires embracing "full-spectrum policing" where police can quickly shift from individual community policing duties into a formed unit (contact or fire teams and squads for close quarters battle) for tactical engagements against an armed and organized opposing force.

While nobody likes to admit it, the very real need for true "combat policing" capability beyond SWAT focused training that pertains to stacked tactics against one or two lightly armed and reactive barricade suspects now exists. Initially, capability gap concerns were expressed pertaining to al-Qaeda and al-Qaeda inspired operations taking place on U.S. soil, along with later Hezbollah linked terrorist potentials with some of these concerns drawn from the Beslan middle school massacre that took place in September 2004 and resulted in the death and injury of hundreds of children.[84] Recent examples of Mexcian cartel linked incidents in the United States that have prompted such needs being discussed include the November 2011 incidents in which a three-vehicle Zetas commando got into a firefight with law enforcement near Houston, TX, and several U.S. SWAT teams were deployed against over a dozen armed cartel and gang members who had crossed the border near Escobares, TX, after fleeing from a Mexican military offensive.[85]

These new capabilities are needed in Mexico, throughout Latin America, and here in the United States. To date, Mexico's Federal police have been building a force structure that emphasizes the tactical gendarmerie-type skill set over the community police capabilities needed to sustain urban security. Development of the full range of police capacity, at all levels of the Mexican state (federal, state, and municipal), is essential. It goes without saying that such capacity must be corruption-free. This necessitates sustained police reform and significant capacity building.

The hybrid skills demanded by "full spectrum policing" would benefit from enhanced law enforcement-military interaction for assessing emerging conflict, developing tactical and operational doctrine, and cross training. It is not simply a matter of bringing counterinsurgency (COIN) skills to the police service, but rather a reciprocal exchange of knowledge and experience to address "inter-conflict policing" where community policing and COIN converge to address the intersection of crime and war. At the strategic level, there is a need to define the role of police-military interaction for convergent threats such as transnational organized crime, criminal insurgency, and crime in conflict zones. This may require new force structures (such as expeditionary police), as well as integrating existing capacities (such as formulating the traditional Diplomatic, Intelligence, Military, and Economic [DIME] as DIME-P, adding the police service). Building an adaptive response capacity to address urban terrorist tactics — including car bombs — employed in the criminal insurgencies now occurring in Mexico and parts of Central America is essential.[86] This requires more than explosive ordnance disposal (EOD) or bomb squad responses. Explosives and ambush awareness must be integrated into all police and emergency (fire/EMS; emergency medical services) response at the general service (patrol, first response) levels in the United States and Latin America. The lessons learned in countering car bombs and IEDs in Iraq and Afghanistan, and now Mexico, must be shared and integrated into evolving public safety doctrine and emerging police operational art.

Derived from the future cartel car bombing potentials identified for Mexico, and also those potentials as they pertain to U.S. personnel and facilities on both sides of the border, and the preceding conclusions reached concerning the need for "full-spectrum policing" with the inclusion of a developed "combat-policing" capability, some initial response recommendations will be suggested. These response recommendations will be focused upon how the U.S. Army and the broader U.S. defense community—which have had recent extensive experience with IEDs, car bombs, and terrorist and insurgent tactics in the Iraqi and AfPak areas of operation—can better support both: a) the military and the federal, state, and local police agencies of the Mexican state; and, b) the various U.S. federal, state, and local police agencies operating near the U.S.-Mexican border:

These recommendations will be clustered into four thematic areas and will be generalized for both internal Mexican and U.S. border region requirements. The extent to which these forms of support may be provided should be considered situational and based on a determinaiton of need derived from the severity of the car bombing, and overall Mexican cartel, threat projected. These initial recommendations for U.S. Army and defense community support are as follows:

- *Intelligence.* The basic historical overview of Colombian and Mexican cartel VBIED (and IEDs in cars) incidents and the indications and warnings (I&W) discussion prior to the resumption of a new wave of car bombings in Mexico can be greatly expanded upon via the use of information beyond that provided by open source intelligence (OSINT). Such information, and the military intelligence process behind it that focuses on futures and enemy intent—rather than backwards looking criminal intelligence that attempts to link a perpetrator in time and space back to a specific crime—is vital for both Mexican and U.S law enforcement to better understand and plan for a tactical and operational environment in which car bombs, IEDs, and infantry weapons utilized by cartel and gang members exist. The National Ground Intelligence Center (NGIC), a component of United States Army Intelligence and Security Command (USAISC), would be a natural candidate for this tasking, as potentially would be the U.S. Army Foreign Military Studies Office (FMSO) with its non-state threat analysis—though the intelligence training and products produced would be required to be at the unclassified, yet limited distribution/sensitive and non-restriction on use OSINT levels for law enforcement utilization.

- *Organization.* Past law enforcement organizational emphasis has focused on tactical level applications—typically with either one or two officers assigned to a patrol car. SWAT teams in smaller cities and towns are considered a collateral duty, as opposed to dedicated teams in major cities, and at best will typically be composed of a 4-5 man fire team or roughly a 11-man squad equivalent unit with more advanced teams fielding a combat medic. In rural policing situations, a lone deputy can be expected to cover a wide geographic area and will be the first on scene to active shooter (agressor) incidents with no backup for long periods of time. For U.S. law enforcement to begin to gain an upper tier 'combat-policing' capability in the face of Mexican cartel threats, new organizational policing forms need to be explored. For border law enforcement found in the larger cities, this would likely include platoon size (3 squads) manuever elements. Further, SWAT, bomb squad, and air resources integrated together will be required to mitigate some potential threat scenarios involving cartel kill-teams integrated with IEDs and/or car bomb deployment. Swarming principals—derived from the work of John Arquilla—which are influencing U.S. Department of Defense organizational thinking also provide immediate utility for U.S and Mexican law enforcement, especially in more rural areas where law enforcement officers will respond to an incident in a hasty and adhoc manner.[87] Hence, the U.S. Army Training and Doctrine Command (TRADOC) would be of immense benefit in providing organizational support thinking to law enforcement on both sides of the border.

- *Training*. Law enforcement is used to functioning in an operational environment characterized by that of crime—not one characterized by conflict and war. As a result, law enforcement officers on both sides of the border do not normally understand military concepts, much less perceptions of an opposition force (OPFOR) that engages in proactive offensive operations, drawing upon both physical and psychological forms of violence, designed to eliminate armed organized resistance. Further, both authors have trained rooms full of law enforcement officers who, save for some reserve and former military personnel, were unable to identify basic military weaponry such as 40mm grenades for the U.S. M203 grenade launcher or understand common military acronyms such as OODA loops or OPSEC. Service and joint programs, such as U.S. Army Training and Doctrine Command and the Joint IED Defeat Organization (JIEDDO), can provide both basic training in such areas as *IED/Car Bomb/Infantry Weapons Awareness, Basic Infantry Tactics/Force Protection,* and *Counterintelligence/OPSEC* for general law enforcement units and more specific training on topics such as *Insurgent IED/Car Bomb TTPs/ Countermeasures* for bomb squad personnel.

U.S. SWAT teams, in some jurisdictions, are also now benefiting from MACTAC (Multi-Assault Counter-Terrorism Action Capabilities) training that is military inspired. This training, when combined with a grounding in the use of the U.S. Army Standard 9-line UXO Report and counter-IED awarness, would significantly help promote increased SWAT capability against VBIED and ambush derived IED threats.

- *Equipment.* Over a decade of U.S. Army campaigning in Iraq and Afghanistan has provided the organization with an intimate knowledge of IEDs, car bombs, and other insurgent ambush techniques. Specific equipment requirements and a vetting of COTS (commercial off-the-shelf) products from lessons learned and paid in the blood of our service personnel has resulted in a wealth of expertise that can be directly provided to Mexican and U.S. law enforcement agencies to support their procurement needs. The best route for coordinated U.S. law enforcement support would be via the InterAgency Board (IAB) for Equipment Standardization and Interoperability, which has a special emphasis on Chemical, Biological, Radiological, Nuclear, or Explosive (CBRNE) issues. The Joint IED Defeat Organization (JIEDDO) should also have a direct role in supporting this process. Support to Mexican governmental authorities should be directed through SEDENA (*Secretaría de la Defensa Nacional*) for the Army and Air Force and through SEMAR (*Secretaría de Marina*) for the Navy. Both armed forces are actively engaging the cartels, with the Army being used for stability and support operations and the Navy primary engaging in more specialized operations against the cartel leadership. U.S. military equipment support to Mexican law enforcement, however, will be more problematic, with currently two federal agencies, 31 state agencies, and well over 1,500 municipal agencies existing.

Reappraisal of the Posse Comitatus Act of 1878 — enacted in a far different domestic security environment bereft of armed and organized nonstate threat entities able to challenge states — is also required if we are to lift some legal restrictions on U.S. military support to U.S. law enforcement agencies.[88] These recommendations, will, of course, also be required to be integrated and subordinated to ongoing U.S. initiatives and programs — such as Mérida Initiative and follow-on congressional authorizations — and ongoing U.S. domestic law enforcement support operations initiated by the DEA, elements of the Department of Homeland Security (DHS), the Federal Bureau of Investigation (FBI), and other U.S. governmental agencies.[89]

Addressing the challenges posed by cartel *sicarios* is a hemispheric security challenge. In addition to internal U.S. military efforts and U.S. support to Mexican military (both SEDENA and SEMAR) and law enforcement (at all levels: federal, state, and municipal), support should also be extended to Central American states facing cartel and gang challenges. An important initiative in this regard is the dramatic increase in senior leader engagements and Subject Matter Expert Exchanges (SMEE)/Mobile Training Team (MTT) activities between the Mexico branch of US Army North's (ARNORTH) Security Cooperation Division and SEDENA. These engagements and activities have gone from three in FY 2009 to 98 in FY 2012.[90]

Additionally, Mexican security agencies (the afforementioned military and police, as well as CISEN-*Centro de Investigación y Seguridad Nacional*, the PGR-*Procuraduría General de la República*, and state prosecutors) need the knowledge and skills to recognize, avoid, or contain; safely respond to; and render safe car bombs and other IEDs. They also need the forensic science skills to investigate car bomb crime scenes and prepare cases for prosecution. It is not enough to transfer skills to the military. Local responders are potential targets of attack and likely the first to respond to a bomb scene. Police and other local level responders (emergency medical services), the Cruz Rojo Mexicana (Mexican Red Cross), and *bomberos* firefighters need the skills to safely respond to, contain, and investigate car bomb attacks. This requires comprehensive civil-military security sector support.

Ultimately, a comprehensive U.S. Northern Command (USNORTHCOM) strategy should be developed in coordination with the Mexican government that integrates all elements of national power to mitigate and counter Mexican cartel use of car bombs and other forms of violence and corruption manifesting themselves in Mexico and increasingly in the United States. To best serve our national interests, however, this comprehensive strategy should also be integrated with the U.S. Southern Command (USSOUTHCOM) to create a Western Hemispheric strategy to combat gang, cartel, and other criminal insurgent threats to the Americas.[91]

ENDNOTES

1. Felipe Calderón, *Cuatro Informe De Gobierno* (4th Governance Report), Mexican Federal Government, Mexico City, Mexico, September 2010, available from *translate.google.com/ translate?hl=en&sl=es&u=cuarto.informe.calderon.presidencia.gob. mx/resumen-ejecutivo/&prev=/search%3Fq%3Dcalderon%2Binforme %2B2010%26hl%3Den%26safe%3Doff%26client%3Dfirefox-a%26hs %3DfRH%26rls%3Dorg.mozilla:en*, English translation.

2. *Ibid.*; Ken Ellingwood, "Mexico's Crackdown on Organized Crime Is Working, Calderón Says." *Los Angeles Times*, September 2, 2010, available from *articles.latimes.com/2010/sep/02/world/la-fg-mexico-informe-20100902*.

3. General elections were subsequently held in Mexico on July 1, 2012, with the PRI candidate Enrique Peña Nieto winning the presidential election. He assumed office on December 1, 2012.

4. Calderón, *Cuatro Informe De Gobierno.*

5. Associated Press, "Drug War: 2 Bodies Hung from Bridge on Road to Acapulco," *Daily Breeze*, August 24, 2010, available from *www.dailybreeze.com/ci_15880607?source=pkg*; E. Eduardo Castillo and Mark Steveson, "Drug Cartel Suspected in Massacre of 72 Migrants," Associated Press, August 26, 2010.

6. John P. Sullivan, "Explosive Escalation? Reflections on the Car Bombing in Ciudad Juarez," *Small Wars Journal*, July 21, 2010, available from *smallwarsjournal.com/blog/2010/07/explosive-escalation/*.

7. The chapter in Davis provides the best overview of Colombian cartel bombings, though, it is still very limited in nature. See "Los Coches Bomba," Mike Davis, *Buda's Wagon: A Brief History of the Car Bomb*, London, UK: Verso, 2007, pp. 108-115.

8. See RAND Database of Worldwide Terrorism Incidents (RDWTI), Santa Monica, CA: RAND, available from *smapp.rand.org/rwtid/search.php*; and Global Terrorism Database (GTD), National Consortium for the Study of Terrorism and Responses to Terrorism, University Park, MD: University of Maryland, available from *www.start.umd.edu/gtd/search*.

9. The Global Terrorism Database (GTD) yielded one unique cartel car bombing in Table 1 compiled for this Paper. Neither database contained most of the major car bombings incidents highlighted. Further attempts to identify actual car bombing incidents in the GTD is extremely tedious.

10. Ron Chepesiuk, *Drug Lords: The Rise and Fall of the Cali Cartel*, Wrea Green Preston, UK: Milo Books Ltd., 2003.

11. Davis, p. 110.

12. Chepesiuk, *Drug Lords*, pp. 134-136.

13. Davis, pp. 111-112.

14. Chepesiuk, *Drug Lords*, p. 129.

15. *Ibid.*

16. Ron Chepesiuk, *The Bullet or the Bribe: Taking Down Colombia's Cali Drug Cartel*, Westport, CT: Praeger, 2003, p. 129; and Alan Riding, "Gangs in Colombia Feud Over Cocaine," *New York Times*, August 23, 1988.

17. The GTD contains many of these incidents but only in fragmentary form.

18. Some potential historical cartel bombing incident information may reside with the New York and Miami-Dade police departments and/or within the institutional memory of some retired Bomb Squad personnel, but such information would not be made available to the public.

19. Billy Corben, director, *Cocaine Cowboys*, DVD, Rakontur Film Venture One LLC and Magnolia Home Entertainment, Los Angeles, CA: Corben, 2005. Ayala is serving multiple life sentences for the cartel killings in which he was involved. In a deleted interview scene, he explained how he learned in Miami to use bombs composed of sticks of dynamite, detonator, wires, battery, and a timer. See deleted scene 8, "Rivi Guns and Bombs."

20. Numerous keyword searches for car bomb use were conducted, including those in the newspaper archives of the *New York Times* and *Miami Herald*.

21. Davis, p. 114.

22. Robert J. Bunker and John P. Sullivan, "Cartel Evolution: Potentials and Consequences," *Transnational Organized Crime*, No. 4, Summer 1998, pp. 55-74. Note that in June 1995, the Cali cartel detonated a car bomb at a music festival, killing at least 30 and wounding 200. This was undertaken as an act of desperation as the Cali cartel was in the process of being eliminated, and one of its leaders, Gilberto Rodriguez Orejuela, had recently been captured. See Davis, p. 115.

23. *Ibid.* Ultimately, Pablo Escobar turned on many of his old associates who were taken to the *La Cathedral* prison and subsequently tortured and killed. Those associates not killed by Pablo, and the surviving family members of those killed by him, increasingly turned against him. See Chepesiuk, *Drug Lords*, pp. 152-153; and Mark Bowden, *Killing Pablo*, New York: Penguin, 2002, p. 118.

24. The Medellin cartel also blew up Avianca Flight 203, killing all 107 passengers aboard in November 1989, as part of an assassination plot, and the Cali cartel attempted to launch an opera-

tion in 1992 in which bombs would be dropped on Pablo Escobar from an airplane while he was in *La Cathedral* prison. Each incident reinforces the mass violence and more discriminate violence tendencies of these warring cartels.

25. This incident centered on Colombian cartel violence tied back to Griselda Blanco and others. The shooters at the mall escaped in a "war wagon" (a truck with steel plating, gun muzzle slots, hanging police-issue body armor for added protection, and 14 weapons) that they later abandoned. See Guy Gugliotta and Jeff Leen, *Kings of Cocaine*, New York: Simon and Schuster, 1989, pp. 9-16; and the film by Corben.

26. Brian Jenkins and Janera Johnson, *International Terrorism: Chronology (1974 Supplement)* R-1909-1-ARPA, Santa Monica, CA: RAND, February 1976, p. 7.

27. Anonymous, "Wave of Anarchist Bombings Strikes Mexico." *Infoshop News*, October 6, 2009, available from *news.infoshop. org/article.php?story=20091006142457315*; Associated Press, "IBM, McDonald's Bombed in Mexican Capital; Leftists Take Responsibility," *Los Angeles Times*, August 16, 1991, available from *articles. latimes.com/1991-08-16/news/mn-604_1_mexico-city*; Jose Rodríguez, "Bombings in Mexico — A Sign of Upcoming Unrest?" *Mexidata.info*, n.d.; and Tracy Wilkinson, "Mexico City Blast Sparks Fears Violence Will Spread," *Los Angeles Times*, January 9, 1994, available from *articles.latimes.com/1994-01-09/news/mn-10200_1_ mexico-city-blast*.

28. A terrorism database search from January 1, 1968, on with the keywords "Mexico" and "Bombing" was conducted using the RDWTI with 52 record matches. A GTD search was also conducted from 1970 to the present. The search criteria were all incidents regardless of doubt, weapons (explosives/bombs/dynamite), attacks (bombing/explosion), and country (Mexico), with 84 incident results. The RDWTI provides superior summaries of the incidents.

29. RDWTI, July 17, 1972, Unknown, Mexico (Record 1).

30. RDWTI, November 8, 1974, Unknown, Mexico (Record 18).

31. RDWTI, April 26, 1986, Commando Internacionalista Simon Bolivar, Mexico (Record 35).

32. Malcolm Beith, *The Last Narco*, New York: Grove Press, 2010, p. 73. Incident not listed in RDWTI or GTD datasets.

33. Times Wire Services, "Car Bomb at Mexico Hotel Kills 5; Drug Link Suspected," *Los Angeles Times*, June 12, 1994, available from *articles.latimes.com/1994-06-12/news/mn-3431_1_drug-link-suspected*. This incident is listed with only fragmentary information as GTD ID:199406130001. No subsequent car bomb entries for either the RDWTI or GTD datasets exist after this date.

34. Barnard R. Thompson, "The Mexican Drug War: Is It 'Narcoterrorism'" (Reprinted from *www.mexidata.info*), *Open Democracy*, August 17, 2010, available from *www.opendemocracy. net/barnard-r-thompson/mexican-drug-war-is-it-narcoterrorism*.

35. This mistake cost the Tijuana cartel dearly and required massive bribes to be paid to Mexican government and law enforcement officials to ensure the integrity of the cartel's leadership and operations. See Robert J. Caldwell, "Cartel Secrets: Top-Level Insider Reveals the Cartel's Most Guarded Info," *The San Diego Union-Tribune*, July 1, 2007, available from *www.signonsandiego. com/uniontrib/20070701/news_lz1e1cartel.html*.

36. Associated Press, "Police: Crude Car Bomb Found at Mexico Shopping Center," *AP Wordstream*, August 18, 2005, available from *www.highbeam.com/doc/1P1-112252641.html*.

37. GTD, 04/12/2006, ID 200604120013 and GTD, 08/24/2006, ID 200608240006.

38. Dudley Althaus and Marion Lloyd, "Homemade Bomb Explodes in Mexico City, Killing Man," *Houston Chronicle*, February 16, 2010, available from *www.chron.com/disp/story.mpl/world/5546550.html*.

39. Ioan Grillo, "Is Mexico's Drug War Escalating?" *Time*, February 19, 2008, available from *www.time.com/time/world/article/0,8599,1714490,00.html*; and STRATFOR, "El Patron and the IED," *Mexico Security Memo*, March 3, 2008.

40. GTD, 09/15/2008, ID 200809150001.

41. Robin Emmott and Ignacio Alvarado, "Mexico Drug Traffickers Make Car Bombs," *Reuters*, July 16, 2008, available from *uk.reuters.com/article/idUKN1652282020080716.*

42. *Ibid.*

43. Additionally, 101 grenade attacks against government buildings have taken place during the last 3 1/2 years, according to the Mexican attorney general's office. Nick Miroff and William Booth, "Mexican Drug Cartels' Newest Weapon: Cold War-Era Grenades Made in U.S.," *The Washington Post*, July 17, 2010.

44. Sullivan, "Explosive Escalation?"

45. *Ibid.*

46. See Scott Stewart, "The Perceived Car Bomb Threat in Mexico," STRATFOR, April 13, 2011.

47. Davis, pp. 1-3.

48. "Mexico Drug Traffickers Make Car Bombs," *Reuters*, July 16, 2008, available from *uk.reuters.com/article/2008/07/16/uk-mexico-drugs-idUKN1652282020080716.*

49. CNN, "Car Bomb Rocks Government Offices in Tamaulipas, Mexico," August 6, 2010, available from *edition.cnn.com/2010/WORLD/americas/08/05/mexico.bomb/#fbid=ytam6KHKbli&wom=false*; and "Car Bomb Blast in Northern Mexico, No Deaths," *Reuters*, August 5 , 2010, available from *www.reuters.com/article/2010/08/06/us-mexico-drugs-idUSTRE67505J20100806.*

50. "Two Car Bombs Explode in Northern Mexico But No Casualties," *Reuters*, August 27, 2010; and Center for Journalism and Public Ethics, "Car Bomb Explodes Outside Tamaulipas Televisa Offices," August 30, 2010, available from *www.ifex.org/mexico/2010/08/30/televisa_tamaulipas_car_bomb/.*

51. Scott Stewart, "The Perceived Car Bomb Threat in Mexico," STRATFOR, April 13, 2011.

52. *Borderland Beat*, "2 car bombs explode in NL," January 18, 2011 [Original sources *Milenio/El Norte*], available from *www. borderlandbeat.com/2011/01/car-bomb-explodes-in-nl.html*; *Borderland Beat*, "Car Bomb Wounds 5 in Northeastern Mexico," March 16, 2011 [Original source *EFE*], available from *www.borderlandbeat. com/2011/03/car-bomb-wounds-5-in-northeastern.html*; *Borderland Beat*, "Car Bomb Disarmed in Ciudad Juarez," September 12, 2010 [Original sources *El Paso Times*, *El Diario de Cd Juarez*, and *El Agora de Chihuahua*, available from *www.borderlandbeat.com/2010/09/car-bomb-disarmed-in-ciudad-juarez.html*; *Borderland Beat*, "Car Bomb Disrupts Diez y Seis Celebration in Tamaulipas State Capitol," September 16, 2011 [Original sources *Milenio/El Norte*], available from *www.borderlandbeat.com/2011/09/car-bomb-disrupts-diez-y-seis. html*; *Borderland Beat*, "Monterrey: Army Attacked in Car Bomb Ambush," October 20, 2011 [Original source *El Norte*], available from *www.borderlandbeat.com/2011/10/monterrey-army-attacked-in-car-bomb.html*; *Borderland Beat*, "Car Bomb Explodes in Zuazua, Nuevo Leon; Communication Threatens 11 More," December 18, 2010 [Original source Mexican news broadcast], available from *www.borderlandbeat.com/2010/12/car-bomb-explodes-in-zua-zua-nuevo-leon.html*; and Emmanuel Rincón, "El coche-bomba en Hidalgo, venganza de los '*Zetas*' contra la policía" ("The Car Bomb in Noble, Revenge of the 'Zeds' Against the Police"), *Excelsior*, January 22, 2011, available from *www.excelsior.com.mx/index. php?m=nota&id_nota=706729&rss=1*.

53. Robert Bunker, "Mexican Cartel Tactical Note #5: Indications & Warning (I&W): VBIED Anti-Vehicular/Anti-Personnel Ambush Capability for Los Zetas Assumed," *Small Wars Journal*, October 24, 2011, available from *smallwarsjournal.com/blog/mexican-cartel-tactical-note-5*.

54. Note: About 10 sticks of explosives are evident in a Mexican Federal police photo. Sergio Chapa, "Car Found with Trunk Full of Explosives in Ciudad Victoria," *ValleyCentral.com*, January 10, 2012, available from *www.valleycentral.com/news/story.aspx?l ist=~%5Cnews%5Clists%5Crecent&id=706076#.UKKQXrT3C9Y*. See also EFE, "Explota un coche bomba frente a diario Expreso en Tamaulipas, norte de México" ("It Exploits a Car Bomb Set Against Newspaper I Express in Tamaulipas, North of Mexico"), *Univision*, March 20, 2012, available from *feeds.univision.com/feeds/ article/2012-03-20/explota-un-coche-bomba-frente*.

55. "Car Bomb Explodes Outside Newspaper Offices in Northern Mexico," *NBCNews.com*, March 20, 2012, available from *worldnews.nbcnews.com/_news/2012/03/20/10769925-car-bomb-explodes-outside-newspaper-offices-in-northern-mexico?lite*. For the Mexican governmental statement, see "communicado de la secretaria de seguridad publica del estado" ("Communication of the Secretary of Seguridad publishes of the State"), March 19, 2012, available from *tamaulipas.gob.mx/2012/03/comunicado-de-la-secretaria-de-seguridad-publica-del-estado-6/*.

56. "Reafirma El Chapo presencia en Tamaulipas con coche bomba" ("It Reaffirms The I Veneer Presence in Tamaulipas with Car Bomb"), *Blog Del Narco*, Martes, April 24, 2012; and News staff, "Car Bomb Explosion Followed By Shootout in Nuevo Laredo," *ValleyCentral.com*, April 24, 2012, available from *www.valleycentral.com/news/story.aspx?id=745672#.UKPaq7T3C9Z*.

57. News staff, "Photos of Damage from Hotel Car Bombing in Nuevo Laredo," *ValleyCentral.com*, May 24, 2012, available from *www.valleycentral.com/news/story.aspx?id=758095#.UKPn4bT3C9Y*; Chris Covert, "10 Wounded in Attack in Nuevo Laredo," *Borderland Beat*, May 24, 2012, available from *www.borderlandbeat.com/2012/05/10-wounded-in-attack-in-nuevo-laredo.html*; and "Estalla coche bomba en Nuevo Laredo; 8 policías y 2 civiles resultaron heridos" ("Car bomb Explodes in New Laredo; 8 Police Officers and 2 Civilians Turned Out to Be Injured"), *La Jornada*, May 25, 2012, p. 16, available from *www.jornada.unam.mx/2012/05/25/politica/016n1pol*.

58. Sergio Chapa, "Double Car Bombing Rocks Ciudad Victoria," *ValleyCentral.com*, June 6, 2012, available from *www.valleycentral.com/news/story.aspx?id=762886#.UKPyMrT3C9Y*.

59. Jason Buch, "Car Bomb Rocks Nuevo Laredo," *MySanAntonio.com*, June 29, 2012, available from *www.mysanantonio.com/news/local_news/article/Car-bomb-rocks-Nuevo-Laredo-3673813.php*; and EFE, "Car Bomb Wounds 7 in Mexican Border City," *Fox News Latino*, June 29, 2012, available from *latino.foxnews.com/latino/news/2012/06/29/car-bomb-wounds-7-in-mexican-border-city/*.

60. "Two Killed in Car Bomb in Mexico; Second Such Attack in a Week," *Los Angeles Times*, July 3, 2012, available from *latimes-blogs.latimes.com/world_now/2012/07/two-killed-car-bomb-mexico.html*; and Associated Press, "Mexico Car Bomb Kills 2 Policemen Outside Home of Top Police Official," *Huffington Post*, July 3, 2012, available from *www.huffingtonpost.com/2012/07/03/mexico-car-bomb-kills_n_1646862.html*.

61. "Mexico: Car Bomb Explodes in Gas Station," *Inforsurhoy*, August 2, 2012, available from *infosurhoy.com/cocoon/saii/xhtml/en_GB/newsbriefs/saii/newsbriefs/2012/08/02/newsbrief-02*. Original news sources: *AFP*, January 8, 2012; *Jornada.unam.mx (Mexico)*, January 8, 2012.

62. Covert, "10 wounded in attack in Nuevo Laredo."

63. Ildefonso Ortiz, "Increased Use of Car Bombs in Tamaulipas Disturbing, Former U.S. Agent Says," *Latino Times*, July 19, 2012.

64. Fred Burton, "Mexican Cartel Bombmaking: Intent vs. Capability (Tearline)," STRATFOR, Video, 3:33 minutes, July 18, 2012, available from *www.stratfor.com/video/mexican-cartel-bomb-making-intent-vs-capability-tearline*.

65. Ioan Grillo, "In Juarez Car Bomb, A Ruthless Trap for Police: Raids on American-Owned Explosives Could Be Behind Sophisticated Car Bomb," *Global Post*, July 26, 2010, available from *www.globalpost.com/dispatch/mexico/100723/ciudad-juarez-car-bomb*.

66. Stewart, "The Perceived Car Bomb Threat in Mexico," pp. 4-5.

67. Robert J. Bunker and John P. Sullivan, *Suicide bombings in Operation Iraqi Freedom*, Land Warfare Paper No. 46W, Arlington, VA: Institute of Land Warfare, Association of the United States Army, September 2004, available from *www3.ausa.org/webpub/DeptILW.nsf/byid/KCAT-6E4LEH*.

68. Patrick Corcoran "Salvadoran Defense Minister Says Stolen Grenades Were for the Zetas," *InSight Crime*, June 27, 2011, available from *www.insightcrime.org/news-briefs/salvadoran-defense-minister-says-stolen-grenades-were-for-the-zetas*.

69. Nick Miroff and William Booth, "Mexican Drug Cartels' Newest Weapon: Cold War-Era Grenades Made in U.S.," *Washington Post*, July 17, 2010, available from *www.washingtonpost.com/wp-dyn/content/article/2010/07/16/AR2010071606252.html*.

70. A number of photos of these weapons seized from the Mexican cartels exist. For examples of forensic analysis, see David A. Kuhn and Robert J. Bunker, "Mexican Cartel Tactical Note #10: Claymore Anti-Personnel Mine (and Other Military Hardware) Recovered in Zacatecas," *Small Wars Journal – El Centro*, May 14, 2012, available from *smallwarsjournal.com/blog/mexican-cartel-tactical-note-10*; and David Kuhn and Robert Bunker, "Mexican Cartel Tactical Note #12: Forensics of Recovered Weapons from Piedras Negras Tactical Engagement Between Los Zetas and GATE (Grupo de Armas y Tácticas Especiales)," *Small Wars Journal – El Centro*, May 31, 2012, available from *smallwarsjournal.com/blog/mexican-cartel-tactical-note-12*.

71. Scott Stewart, "The Buffer Between Mexican Cartels and the U.S. Government," STRATFOR, August 17, 2011, available from *www.stratfor.com/weekly/20110817-buffer-between-mexican-cartels-and-us-government#ixzz2CJvvNfwJ*. Also see note #22, where the Cali cartel willingly broke this firebreak out of sheer desperation.

72. "EU amuralla consulado en Monterrey" ("EU Consulate Walls in Monterrey"), *El Universal*, April 5, 2011, available from *www.eluniversal.com.mx/estados/80020.html*. A grenade had been thrown at the consulate in October 2008 and near it later in October 2010. Nick Valencia, "Grenades Explode Near U.S. Consulate in Mexico," *CNN*, October 2, 2010, available from *articles.cnn.com/2010-10-02/world/mexico.us.consulate.blasts_1_consulate-mexican-officials-grenades?_s=PM:WORLD*.

73. The official Mexican governmental death toll figure was 47,515 as of January 2012. This figure does not include the tens of thousands of individuals who have simply disappeared and individuals who have been killed in Mexican states that are not reporting cartel related homicides. See Andrew O'Reilly, "Mexico's Drug Death Toll Double What Reported, Expert Argues," Fox News Latino, August 10, 2012, available from *latino.foxnews.com/latino/news/2012/08/10/mexico-drug-death-toll-double-what-reported-*

expert-argues/; and Chivis Martinez, "NARCO HOMICIDES: 'The Real' Number 100-200+ Thousand," *Borderland Beat*, August 19, 2011, available from *www.borderlandbeat.com/2012/08/narco-homicides-real-number-100-200.html*.

74. John P. Sullivan and Adam Elkus, "Tactics and Operations in the Mexican Drug War," *Infantry*, Vol. 100, Issue 4, September-October 2011, pp, 20-23; and John P. Sullivan and Adam Elkus, "Narco-Armor in Mexico," *Small Wars Journal*, July 14, 2011, available from *smallwarsjournal.com/jrnl/art/narco-armor-in-mexico*.

75. Elyssa Pachico, "Tracking the Steady Rise of Beheadings in Mexico," *InSight Crime*, October 28, 2012, available from *www.insightcrime.org/news-analysis/tracking-the-steady-rise-of-beheadings-in-mexico*. See also Marcos Muedano, "Decapitaciones se desatan este sexenio" ("Beheadings Are Unleashed by This Six"), *El Universal*, October 28, 2012, available from *www.eluniversal.com.mx/notas/879375.html*.

76. *National Drug Threat Assessment 2011*, Washington, DC: National Drug Intelligence Center (NDIC), August 2011.

77. For example, see Kimberly Dvorak, "Mexican Drug Cartels Threaten U.S. Border Patrol Agents - Place a Bounty on Their Lives," *Examiner.com*, April 12, 2010, available from *www.examiner.com/article/mexican-drug-cartels-threaten-u-s-border-patrol-agents-place-a-bounty-on-their-lives*.

78. Fortunately, the gang member did not arm the grenade properly prior to throwing it into the bar. The grenade was South Korean made and had the same markings as grenades used against the U.S consulate in Monterey, Mexico, in October 2008. Associated Press, "Cartel Grenades May Be Coming into U.S," *NBCNews.com*, August 3, 2009, available from *www.msnbc.msn.com/id/32272978/ns/us_news-security/t/cartel-grenades-may-be-coming-us/#.UKVW4qX3C9Y*.

79. Fred Burton and Scott Stewart, "Mexican Cartels and the Fallout From Phoenix," STRATFOR, July 2, 2008, available from *www.stratfor.com/weekly/mexican_cartels_and_fallout_phoenix*.

80. For past attacks on U.S. personnel and civilians in Mexico, see Stewart, "The Buffer Between Mexican Cartels and the U.S. Government." Also see the attacks on the CIA personnel and Mexican naval officer that took place in August 2012 on the dirt road known as El Capulin, in Xalatlaco, Mexico State. Chivis, "Mexico City: 2 Ambushed in Mexico City are CIA Agents," *Borderland Beat*, August 29, 2012, available from *www.borderlandbeat. com/2012/08/mexico-city-2-ambushed-in-mexico-city.html*.

81. John Bailey and Matthew M. Taylor, "Evade, Corrupt Or Confront? Organized Crime and the State in Brazil and Mexico," *Journal of Politics in Latin America*, Vol. 1, 2009, pp, 3-29. See also Graham Turbiville, Jr., "Silver Over the Border: US Law Enforcement Corruption on the Southwest Border," *Small Wars & Insurgencies*, Vol. 22, No. 5, pp. 835-859; and *Crossing the Line: Corruption at the Border*, Berkeley, CA: Center for Investigative Reporting, September 2011, available from *projects.cironline.org/ bordercorruption/*.

82. See Barry R. McCaffrey and Robert H. Scales, *Texas Border Security: A Strategic Military Assessment*, Alexandria, VA: COL-GEN Ltd., September 2011, available from *www.mccaffreyassociates.com/wp-content/uploads/2012/05/Final_Report-Texas_Border_Security.pdf*.

83. These concerns have been raised in a number of news reports. See Ildefonso Ortiz, "Increased Use Of Car Bombs In Tamaulipas Disturbing, Former U.S. Agent Says," *Latino Times*, July 19, 2012; and Stewart Powell, "Threat of IEDs Growing at Home," *Mysanantonio.Com*, July 29, 2012, *www.mysanantonio.com/news/local_news/article/Threat-of-IEDs-growing-at-home-3745215.php*.

84. These presentations to U.S. law enforcement draw upon works that include David Grossman, *On Combat*, Belleville, IL: PPCT Research Publications, 2007; and John Giduck, *Terror at Beslan*, Golden, CO: Archangel Group Inc., 2005.

85. Robert Bunker, "Mexican Cartel Tactical Note # 7: Los Zetas Three Vehicle (SUV) Commando Engages in Offensive Action in Northwest Harris County, Texas: Ensuing Fire Fight with US Law Enforcement," *Small Wars Journal*, November 26, 2011, available from *smallwarsjournal.com/blog/mexican-cartel-tactical-note-7;*

and Robert Bunker and Sid Heal, "Mexican Cartel Tactical Note # 6: Cross Border Incursion with SWAT Teams Responding: 15 Cartel/Gang Gunmen Cross into US Near Escobares, Texas," *Small Wars Journal*, November 15, 2011, available from *smallwarsjournal. com/blog/mexican-cartel-tactical-note-6*.

86. These criminal insurgencies are viewed as a situation that is more dire than high intensity crime and that directly challenges state legitimacy and solvency.

87. Dr. John Arquilla is a professor of defense analysis with the Naval Post Graduate School, Monterey, CA. His work focuses on netwar and swarming. See John Arquilla and David Ronfeldt, *Swarming and the Future of Conflict*, Santa Monica, CA: RAND, 2000, available from *www.rand.org/pubs/documented_briefings/ DB311.html*.

88. Powell, "Threat of IEDs growing at home."

89. For instance, out of Texas and California, various forms of Mexican cartel awareness training are being provided to U.S. law enforcement officers. This training, provided via the Los Angeles High Intensity Drug Trafficking Area (LAHIDTA) in coordination with other agencies and groups, has included focusing on ambush tactics used by the Tijuana cartel, saints of the drug underworld, and cartel identification. Current training being offered is available from *www.lahidtatraining.org/*.

90. Brian Woolworth, "Enhancing North American Security through Military to Military Relationships," *Small Wars Journal – El Centro*, November 30, 2012, available from *smallwarsjournal. com/blog/enhancing-north-american-security-through-military-to-military-relationshi*.

91. Calls for such a comprehensive strategy have been made in the past. For example, see the "Recommendation: Establish a multiorganizational (e.g., U.S. Army Staff, U.S. Army War College, Joint Staff, SOUTHCOM, and NORTHCOM, etc.) 'Tiger Team' to develop a regional security plan that includes foundational ways and means to achieve appropriate mindset and organizational change within the U.S. Army"; Dr. Max Manwaring, "The New Security Reality: Not Business as Usual," *Strategic Studies Institute*

Newsletter Op-Ed., August 20, 2012, available from *www.strategic-studiesinstitute.army.mil/index.cfm/articles/The-New-Security-Reality-Not-Business-as-Usual/2012/08/20.* See also the call for a Western Hemispheric strategy in Robert J. Bunker, "Strategic Threat: Narcos and Narcotics Overview," *Small Wars & Insurgencies*, Vol. 21, No. 1, March 2010, pp. 21-24.

www.ingramcontent.com/pod-product-compliance
Lightning Source LLC
Chambersburg PA
CBHW071114280526
45787CB00003B/1043